LET'S EXPLORE JAPAN
(MOST FAMOUS ATTRACTIONS IN JAPAN)

SPEEDY
PUBLISHING

Speedy Publishing LLC
40 E. Main St. #1156
Newark, DE 19711
www.speedypublishing.com

Japan is an island country in East Asia. Japan is often called the "Land of the Rising Sun". Japan is one of the most popular travel destinations in the world.

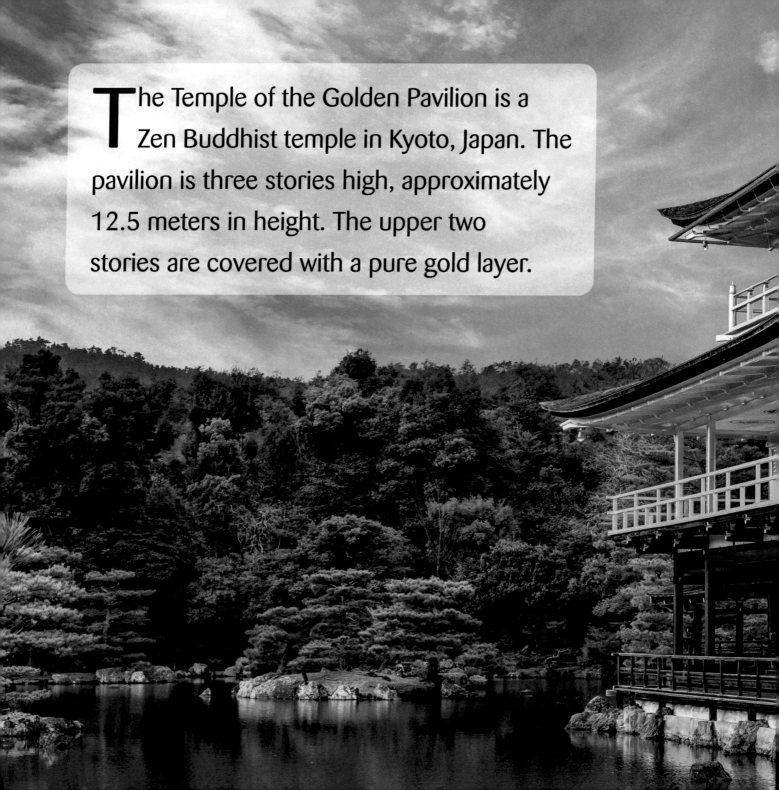

The Temple of the Golden Pavilion is a Zen Buddhist temple in Kyoto, Japan. The pavilion is three stories high, approximately 12.5 meters in height. The upper two stories are covered with a pure gold layer.

Mount Fuji is the highest mountain in Japan. Mount Fuji is made up of three separate volcanoes: Komitake at the bottom, Kofuji at the middle and Fuji at the top.

The Tokyo Imperial Palace is located in Chiyoda, Tokyo. Tokyo Imperial Palace is the main residence of the Emperor of Japan.

Tōdai-ji is a Buddhist temple complex. Once one of the powerful Seven Great Temples, located in the city of Nara, Japan. Tōdai-ji is famous for housing Japan's largest Buddha statue.

J igokudani Monkey Park is located in the valley of the Yokoyu-River. The park is inhabited by Japanese Macaques, which are also known as Snow Monkeys.

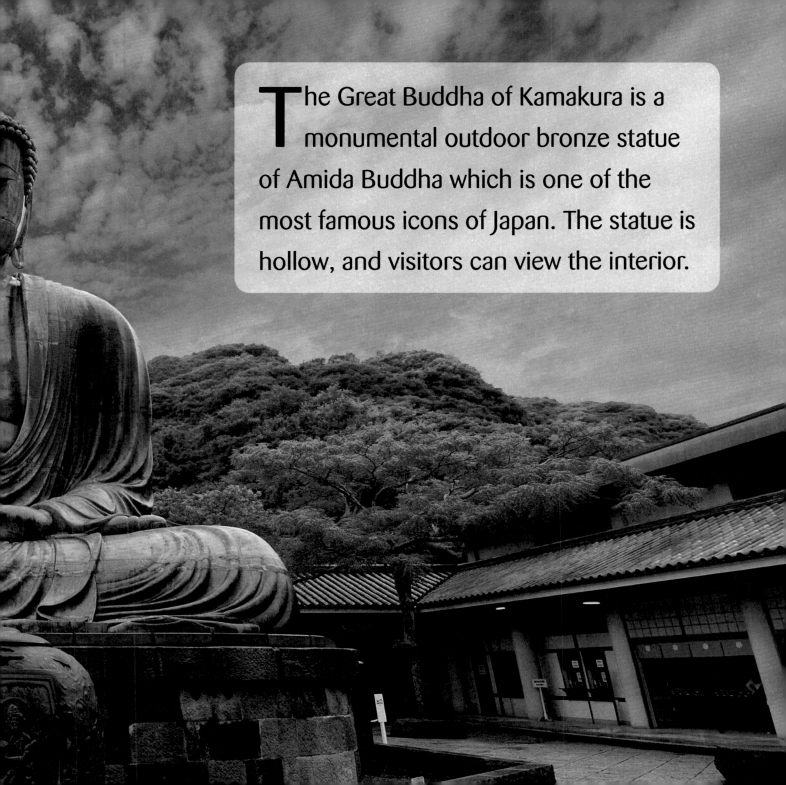

The Great Buddha of Kamakura is a monumental outdoor bronze statue of Amida Buddha which is one of the most famous icons of Japan. The statue is hollow, and visitors can view the interior.

Tokyo Tower is a communications and observation tower located in Tokyo, Japan. It is the second-tallest structure in Japan. Every 5 years the tower is repainted in a process that takes about 12 months.

Made in the USA
San Bernardino, CA
05 April 2016